STEAM MEMORIES ON SHED: 1950's – 1960's

No. 28: NORTH EASTERN SHEDS & T

D Dalton, K Pirt & D Beecroft

Copyright Book Law Publications 2012
ISBN 978-1-907094-87-3

INTRODUCTION

The North Eastern Region of British Railways contained essentially the locomotive sheds originating from the North Eastern Railway. However, in September 1956 those sheds located in the West Riding of Yorkshire and formerly becoming to the London Midland Region (inherited by the LMS from the Lancashire & Yorkshire, London & North Western, and Midland railways) were handed over to the NE Region by dint of boundary changes. Thus, two new groups of engine sheds were created – 55 and 56. The 55 group mainly contained sheds from the old LMS Midland Division but with a couple from the erstwhile Central Division. 56 group encompassed five sheds from the old Central Division and three depots which were once Great Northern in origin. Goole, another former LMS Central Div. shed, became part of the 53 group under Hull. Thus, by February 1957 the North Eastern Region engine shed listing under BR was complete.

This album contains illustrations depicting many of the NE Region depots and their locomotives as they were under BR ownership from Tweedmouth in the north to Hull in the east, and Low Moor in the west of the region.

A number of people helped in supplying photographs whilst other read the manuscript and the compiler would like to thank David Dunn, Ian Trivett, David Allen and John Hooper for their contributions.

Cover Picture (See Page 42)

(previous page) **51F – West Hartlepool, 24th April 1955. This is a view of the south end of the north (straight) shed on another sunny Sunday afternoon in April 1955. This three road building was brought into use in 1867 becoming the first major engine shed at West Hartlepool. It was followed, some four years later, by the first of two square roundhouses built approximately 300 yards to the south, opposite Newburn junction. The third shed, built adjoining the first roundhouse, opened four years later in 1875. Along with a ramped coaling stage, the locomotive facilities at West Hartlepool were now complete and ready for the expansion of both coal mining and the iron and steel industry. Note that the complement of locomotives in view consists entirely of tank engines, all, it appears, being 0-6-0s and a reflection perhaps of the eighty strong allocation which was virtually 50% tank engines. Nearest the camera, J71 No.68244 was one of a dozen of the class maintained at West Hartlepool at this time and used for shunting the yards in the area besides trip working between various industrial premises and the docks. Across the main line is the west wall of the wagon works which turns up in other views of this depot. *K.R.Pirt.***

Printed and bound by The Amadeus Press, Cleckheaton, West Yorkshire
First published in the United Kingdom by Book Law Publications, 382 Carlton Hill, Nottingham, NG4 1JA

53C – The original Hull & Barnsley engine shed at Alexandra Dock, Hull ceased to exist in December 1928 when it was demolished on the grounds of safety! Erected for the opening of the aforementioned dock in 1885, the two road shed was of timber construction and stood at the north-east corner of the enclosed dock alongside the No.1 graving dock, adjacent to the hydraulic engine house. The latter building was of more substantial construction consisting of brick walls with ornamental stone – the lofty tower can be seen behind J73 No.68361 in this view captured on Sunday 24th July 1955. The cost of building the H&B, along with the dock at Hull and its extensive facilities for the export of coal, had virtually wiped out the funds raised for the creation of the railway so the engine shed was regarded as one building where expenditure could be cut back. That the shed remained virtually intact for forty-odd years is testimony to the carpenters who erected it, but the reason for its demise was a distinct leaning of the south wall which was threatening a collapse onto any engines inside the shed, hence demolition. From then on, locomotives stabled out in the open – most of the twenty-odd strong allocation already stood outside anyway because there was only room for about eight engines under cover. This view, taken from the south-east corner of the 'shed' shows a typical mix of the locomotives in use at Alexandra Dock throughout the LNER and BR periods. Identified, from right to left are J73s Nos.68361 and 68360, along with J72s Nos.68676 and 69009. Behind them is a line of diesel-electric shunters which by this date numbered thirteen of the 350 h.p. 0-6-0 type. When the last half dozen steam 0-6-0T departed from the shed in 1960, they were replaced by six 204 h.p. 0-6-0 diesel-mechanical shunting locomotives. In October 1963 the requirement for an independent 'shed' at Alexandra Dock ceased and Dairycoates supplied the motive power from thereon. The Dairycoates based diesels – Botanic supplied them during the 1970s – when not in use, continued to use the stabling roads at Alex' Dock until the commercial dock itself closed in 1982, albeit only to re-open some nine years later. *K.R.Pirt.*

52F sub – By the end of the 19th Century, Blyth, in Northumberland, was blessed with two engine sheds, each located on opposite banks of the river. North Blyth, opened in 1897, was a typical NER square roundhouse constructed to house the engines handling the growing mineral traffic between the coal mines of the expanding coalfield and the shipping staithes built on the north bank of the River Blyth. On the other side of the river, South Blyth engine shed stood adjacent to the passenger station, a terminus known simply as Blyth (closed November 1964) and which stood at the end of a branch line from Newsham; the running lines were just on the extreme left of this 10th April 1955 picture. The six road shed in view dates from 1880 (left hand three roads) and 1894 (right hand roads), the extension being a virtual copy of the original building in most aspects. To the left of the picture can be seen the rectangular shape of the depot's water tank in front of which was the 50ft diameter hand operated turntable. A ramped coaling stage, of typical NER proportions and latterly very dilapidated, stood immediately behind the photographer. Throughout its life the shed was able to house all of its charges and never appeared to be overcrowded unlike some other establishments. As at the North shed, the allocation here consisted about twenty locomotives at any one time (they shared the same shed code throughout the BR ownership – 52F), roughly half being 0-6-0 tender engines, the ubiquitous J27 class holding top position during BR days, although J21 was represented until the demise of that class, whilst G5 and a couple of J77 made up the tank engine contingent. The two J77 were used mainly for shunting the staithes located on the south shore of the river, a job which they had performed successfully for three different owners during their long lives. North shed had five of the powerful 0-6-0 tanks which they also used on their staithes. For those who experienced the sight and sound of the J77 tanks working those staithes, it was something which would never be forgotten. Though some distance apart across the water, the two sets of tank engines seemed to be in competition as to which one could make the most noise propelling the loaded coal wagons up the inclines and onto the staithes. A more genteel existence surrounded the 0-4-4T of G5 class which looked after the passenger services. South Blyth engine shed closed at the end of May 1967 although diesel locomotives continued to stable there for a further twelve months. North Blyth shed was kept open until the end of steam on the NE Region – September 1967! *K.R.Pirt.*

4

One of the South Blyth G5s, the unique No.67340, stables outside the shed on No.3 road on 10th April 1955. Besides the J27 in view, a J25, No.65727 pokes it's smokebox out of the shed and gives us a chance to compare the boiler diameters of the two 0-6-0 classes. The fifty-odd years old G5 was a recent addition to South Blyth's allocation having arrived from Hull during the previous November; this stint at 52F however was not the engine's first because it had spent nine months here pre-WW2. This particular residency was to be the tank's last, although it was to be April 1958 before it was condemned and then cut up at Darlington works. This view of the shed's east gable enables us to see construction details of both sheds; although fourteen years separates the two constructions, it is difficult to spot any difference but they are there for the eagle-eyed. The shed site is now occupied by the Cottage Hospital whilst Blyth station was cleared away to provide space for a Safeway supermarket. For those of you wondering if the wall clock was working on this sunny Sunday in 1955 – yes, the clock was working and it was also keeping correct time! *K.R.Pirt.*

54C & 52J – Borough Gardens engine shed in Gateshead was one of the larger NER sheds comprising four adjacent square roundhouses numbered, from east to west, 1, 2, 3, and 4. We are looking at the south-west wall of No.3 roundhouse on Sunday 22nd May 1955 with a congregation of engines gathered around the two entrance/exit roads serving all four sheds; the left hand track, on which the furthest J39 is standing, served No.3 shed turntable whilst the track virtually hidden by the piles of ash and clinker in the foreground passed through No.3 shed to serve the turntable in No.2 shed! All four tables, which were in line, and their respective stalls were accessible from either of these entrances. Another entrance/exit road penetrated the south corner of No.1 shed. Considering the building could comfortably stable eighty tender engines under cover, Borough Gardens was rarely, if ever, called upon to do so and contrary to the scene illustrated here, the shed was never overcrowded. At Grouping the allocation consisted sixty-odd engines of which a third were 0-8-0s, a third 0-6-0 tank engines, and the rest 0-6-0 tender engines. At Nationalisation the numbers were much the same although the total had dropped to sixty and was starting to recede further. At closure in 1959 some forty-three locomotives remained to be re-allocated elsewhere. J39 class leader No.64700, along with two others of its ilk, simmer in the late morning sunshine during their weekend respite from the incessant weekday workings moving mineral trains around Tyneside. These 0-6-0s of the LNER Standard classes were latecomers to Borough Gardens and only arrived in BR days to replace to dwindling numbers of Class J24 and J25. *K.R.Pirt.*

Seen on the same Sunday as the engines in the previous photograph, one of Borough Gardens larger residents, Q6 No.63342, has its fire tended whilst it heads the line of locomotives ready for the early morning departures on Monday. This long standing member of the Borough Gardens allocation (it had transferred from Newport during December 1943) moved on to Consett when the shed closed in June 1959 but actually ended its days at Sunderland, in December 1963. *K.R.Pirt.*

The outside stabling roads at Borough Gardens shed on an April Sunday in 1956 with Raven, Gresley and Thompson designs on display – J39 No.64700 is prominent along with B1 No.61321. With eighty stalls available inside the roundhouses it seems inconceivable that these engines should be stuck outside when, on paper at least, the whole allocation could be accommodated inside. The reservation for outside stabling had however been installed some years before by the North Eastern with the knowledge that certain classes then being introduced would not fit on all of the shed's turntables. However, Borough Gardens shed was also used for the seasonal storage of A8s, G5s and V3s – all under cover. Smoke nuisance has been kept to a minimum, the Borough Gardens fire watchers knowing just how to tend the fires to best effect. *David Dalton.*

54D & 52K – Consett Junction engine shed, to give it the North Eastern title, consisted a one road shed which was barely 120 feet long when British Railways came into being. During 1950 a similar sized one-road building, of the same profile, was built on the western side of that 1875-built shed. Combined, the two lines of covered accommodation could just about house four tender engines, hardly enough for the dozen or so 0-8-0s and four N8 tank engines allocated to the place around that time. This view of the depot on 10th June 1956, gives some indication of the situation presented each weekend. The coaling facilities consisted a platform where buckets were loaded by hand from wagons and then hoisted by crane to be tipped into waiting tenders. A turntable had existed once at this place but had been removed even before the Grouping so the resident locomotives went about their daily toil facing whichever way the task took them. All the engines in view are Q6 0-8-0s with Nos.63404, 63427, 63359, and 63372 identifiable. The shed with the wagon sticking out was the 'modern' addition! *David Dalton.*

Q6 No.63404, again at Consett, but it is now Sunday 30th August 1959. This view shows some of the industrial infrastructure of the steelworks which virtually surrounded this shed site. The allocation at Consett had not changed much over the decade of BR ownership but the N8s had gone whilst a few more Q6s had joined the ranks here. Although the Consett steel works received all of its iron ore via Tyne Dock, none of the Consett engines were involved in its transportation from the port; that was the preserve of the Tyne Dock O1s, Q7s and 9Fs until the diesels took over. Consett engine shed closed in May 1965 still with half a dozen Q6 and a newly acquired K1 allocated. Eventually, the steel plants themselves closed and today nothing exists to show what had filled the horizon just over fifty years ago. *David Dalton.*

51A – Sunday morning, 24th April 1955 found these two ex-works 2-6-2Ts on Darlington shed ready for running-in prior to returning home. Nearest is Middlesbrough's V3 No.67686 which had finished a General overhaul on the previous Thursday. Behind is Eastfield based V1 No.67664, which had come off the works on the Saturday morning after undergoing a Heavy Intermediate overhaul. Both engines are coaled and look immaculate. Either by design or coincidence, note that each is pointing in the direction of their intended travel to get back to their respective sheds – perhaps some thought was put into such detail. As LNER No.420, No.67664 started life in 1938 working from sheds in the ex Great Eastern Area and during the next fourteen years it required six boiler changes (two of the lifts saw the same boiler being put back on after refurbishment) but after its transfer to Scotland in 1952 only two changes were needed during its ten year residence there. After a three year spell at Botanic Gardens shed in Hull, No.67686 ended its days at Dairycoates shed and was condemned there in September 1963. No.67664, made redundant by the Glasgow electrification, was sent to the former Glasgow & South Western shed at Hurlford during March 1962 but by the end of that summer period it was put into storage and never worked again. It was condemned in December 1962 but was then laid-up for nearly a year before making its final journey to Darlington for breaking up in October 1963. No.67686 followed two month later. *K.R.Pirt.*

On the same Sunday morning that our V1/V3 sisters enhanced the stabling roads at Darlington shed, A3 No.60078 NIGHT HAWK was making its way around the eastern quadrant of the roundhouse from the coaling plant to a position on the turntable track at the south end of the shed yard to take up duties as main line pilot for the day. Darlington shed had two Gresley A3 Pacifics specifically allocated for the main line pilot job. Stabling on the turntable road throughout the duty, the engine usually faced the Up direction but in the event of an engine failure on a northbound express, the duty Pacific could be quickly turned and sent off to wherever its services were required. No.60078 performed this duty whilst allocated to Darlington from February to August 1955 – the normal six month period for the job. Besides Darlington providing a main line pilot engine around the clock, Doncaster and York were two other centres which had a similar set-up to keep the East Coast main line virtually trouble free from failures! This view on the eastern boundary of Darlington shed allows us a look at the external face of the twenty-stall roundhouse which dated from 1866 and had recently had its roof re-clad, although the turntable inside remained uncovered. The building on the right was the breakdown crane shed. *K.R.Pirt.*

Darlington shed, Sunday 13th December 1964, with Peppercorn A1 No.60124 KENILWORTH acting as main line pilot for the day. The position of the engine would indicate perhaps that it was blocking access to the turntable but another road led onto the table from the shed side – as can be seen, the table is actually set to receive locomotives from that particular road – so the presence of the main line pilot did not impede shed movements. BR appear to have introduced Pacifics onto the Darlington turn at the end of 1948 with two A3s (60070 and 60076) initially employed until January 1952! Obviously those two engines did not run up much in the way of mileage during that three year period. From thereon, a six month rota was brought into play whereby each engine would be allocated for six months and then return to normal main line traffic duties. A number of A3s carried out this job until superseded by A1s towards the end of steam at Darlington. Records show that the following were employed at various times but always for that crucial six month deployment, the figure in brackets indicates the actual number of stints each engine undertook: Nos.60036 (1), 60038 (2), 60040 (5), 60042 (3), 60045 (5), 60051 (3), 60052 (2), 60053 (2), 60058 (2), 60060 (4), 60070 (4), 60071 (5), 60075 (5), 60076 (5), 60078 (1), 60082 (1), 60091 (2). The last A3s employed were Nos.60036 and 60045 which carried the job from December 1963 to November 1964 – twelve months note! This A1 had re-allocated from York just three weeks beforehand to take up this important Darlington turn, and it was to prove to be its last home, besides its final job, as it was condemned on the day that the shed closed on 27th March 1966. The A1 appears to have carried out the duty alone – no doubt the extended reliability of diesel locomotives was beginning to take effect by this time – but it was joined by No.60145 from 2nd January 1966 until the shed closed. Unlike No.60124, No.60145 escaped from 51A afterwards to do other work elsewhere for a short period before it too was withdrawn. Virtually on the spot where the Pacific is standing was the location of the manual coaling stage which stood until the mechanical coaling plant was brought into operation in the 1930s. Note also the contaminated ground around the A1 – sixteen years worth of lubrication had probably made the 'soil' quite flammable. *David Dalton.*

13

Another ex works tank engine takes in the sun at Darlington. This Thompson L1 had travelled from Ipswich for the privilege of being given a General overhaul during the summer of 1955 (22nd July to 10th September) and is ready return home. The date is 18th September, a Sunday, and after a week of running-in at 51A, the 2-6-4T has a nice coating of dust over its week-old but still resplendent lined black livery. *David Dalton.*

Besides all the pristine ex-works engines on shed, Darlington obviously played host to engines about to attend North Road works. The works lines were situated in the north-east corner of the running shed yard where the engines congregated before being hauled dead to the works. V2 No.60932, of Tweedmouth shed, is waiting its turn for entry into the shops during January 1957 – a Heavy Intermediate overhaul was carried out 28th January to 1st March 1957. Its next major overhaul at Darlington, during August 1958, would see separate cylinders fitted; by which time it would have transferred to Heaton. This Doncaster built engine was one of the V2s which ended up at Swindon during 1964, in the most dire of circumstances! *David Dalton.*

52A – J25 No.(6)5658 was withdrawn 17th August 1950 and when this scene was recorded at Gateshead shed in June 1954, it was still wearing its 51J Northallerton shed plate. The engine's only identification was a roughly chalked number on the front sandbox but if someone had bothered to clean the filth off the cabside the number E5658 would have been revealed! When it was condemned it was found that the boiler was still in good condition, a happy coincidence perhaps because Gateshead Greensfield engine shed needed a new boiler for their wash-out and heating requirements. Without further ado the 0-6-0 was taken through the roundhouses to this yard at the west end of the depot next to No.4 roundhouse where, for the next five years, it was put to work after being connected to the depot's pipework. It is uncertain if the J25 relieved another locomotive boiler combination or simply a grounded fixed boiler. However, this duty was undertaken until June 1955 when the boiler, No.3442 which had been put on the engine in February 1948, finally gave out and the whole locomotive was hauled away for scrap. Note the V2 stabled half in and half out of the shed on a stall which normally would only accommodate a tank engine if the doorway had not been located there. *David Dalton.*

Haymarket A3 No.60097, the one with those 'different' smoke deflectors, takes water at the column at the east end of the office block at Gateshead (Greensfield) shed during the afternoon of Thursday 29th September 1955. The Pacific has just worked into Newcastle from Edinburgh and is going through the servicing routine – coal has already been loaded – prior to negotiating the junction at Gateshead East where it could reverse course and run down to Central station to pick-up its northbound train. The dilapidated building in the right background is the locomotive works which at this time was still in business overhauling locomotives for the North Eastern Region. However, its location, alongside the always busy engine shed, made access for both establishments rather difficult and was never ideal. *David Dalton.*

A rather interesting photograph of the interior of Gateshead engine shed on 29th September 1955 as seen from the 48ft electric turntable situated in No.1 roundhouse. This turntable was the smallest of the four employed at this shed – the others were all 60ft diameter – and attracted the smaller engines to its sixteen stalls; witness N10 No.69109 and J72 No.68674. V2 No.60809 is managing to stable on the access track which led from the yard into No.2 shed. Note the column which has been subject to a rather heavy blow from a locomotive being positioned, rather clumsily it appears, into one of the stalls radiating from No.2 turntable. *David Dalton.*

52B – Sunday morning at Heaton coaling stage with a bit of banter being exchanged between the coalmen as they tidy up after filling the tender of ex works K3 No.61805 on 22nd May 1955. The Stratford based 2-6-0 had just completed a General overhaul at Doncaster and was being run-in prior to returning home to the Great Eastern section. It is surprising just how far Doncaster sent their ex-works charges before releasing them back into traffic. No.61805 must have performed as expected because it was sent back to London from 36A that same week. Heaton meanwhile carried on servicing its own 100 plus charges, besides looking after the many visitors. From this point, the K3 would proceed to the ash pits located north of the coaling stage, and once that procedure was completed it would reverse down to the 70ft turntable from where it would go on shed ready for working south when the time approached. Note the lavish number of water columns on the face of the stage – six in total. Besides these water points, Heaton had a somewhat unique system whereby water outlets were employed over each road at the western end of the engine shed, fed from a pipe which spanned all five roads, attached to the gable. The system had been installed in 1931 when that end of the shed was opened out to allow through running. A question which has always puzzled this compiler 'Why did the majority of engine sheds in the old North Eastern area, including many of the busy and large establishments such as Gateshead and Heaton, continue to use these manual coaling stages right up to the end?' *K.R.Pirt.*

The Heaton coaling stage on Sunday 22nd February 1953, with resident J25 No.65656 being replenished. *David Dalton.*

St Margarets K3 No.61983, along with an unidentified J39, and a local V1, stand over one of the two ash pits at Heaton shed in April 1956. Compared with many NER engine sheds, Heaton had a lavish amount of space with all the facilities spread out but, at the same time, laid out in a sequence where conflicting movements were minimal. This is the north end of the yard and in the distance can be seen a Pacific near to the shed outlet at Benton Bank signal box. Note that all the locomotives in view have already visited the coaling stage and are now having their fires cleaned and ash pans emptied. Beyond the 2-6-0, two Pacifics, which have worked in from the south are also having their fires tended. From here all the engines would move down the yard to the turntable; the K3 going through 180 degrees ready for the trip back to Edinburgh, the J38 is already facing north so probably no change in direction required. The adjacent Pacifics would likewise use the turntable. *Ron Hodge.*

Sub to 52C – Seen from the other side of the original 43ft 6in diameter turntable, the two-road engine shed at Hexham, located to the east of Hexham station on the Newcastle to Carlisle main line, was a sub shed of Blaydon. On Friday 23rd May 1958, J21 class No.65103, one of the latter's charges, appears to have a full head of steam as it stables at the east end of the through shed to await its next job. Although no exact date is known for the opening of this shed, there was probably some type of locomotive accommodation from the late 1830s by which time the station was fully working. In 1869 the shed was doubled in size, this was achieved either by lengthening the building or adding another road, again, details are unknown. Nine years later yet another extension took place and the two-road shed was certainly in operation. In circa 1929 a fire destroyed the shed which was rebuilt almost immediately. Then, during World War II, fire engulfed the roof of the shed after a German incendiary landed on the structure. Being some distance from Tyneside, it could be deemed that Hexham engine shed was a somewhat unlucky building and rather than it being a target, it was probably the victim of a dumped bomb load from a homeward bound enemy bomber. The roof and affected sections of the shed walls were later rebuilt to the substantial condition seen here. No further episodes of bad luck occurred and the shed passed into history when it closed during April 1959. However, the building stood undisturbed for twenty years or so afterwards. The sixty-six years old J21 had succumbed during December 1958 but note the vacuum brake and screw coupling for passenger stock working. *David Dalton.*

53B & 50C – Botanic Gardens, Hull, late afternoon, Sunday 15th March 1953. It appears as though the negative is scratched but its actually the Pacific tank which has been 'in the wars'. The A6 has certainly been in contact with a similarly heavy object because the front bufferbeam has taken a knock from more than one angle. Whatever misfortune had befallen No.69796, did it have a bearing on shortening its life because two weeks after this photograph was taken, the 4-6-2 was condemned and taken to Darlington for scrapping! However, No.69796 was the last of its class and perhaps its time was up anyway; it was after all some forty-five years old and had been the sole A6 for more than eighteen months by the time of its withdrawal. During that final year or so, the big engine had been shuttling between Paragon station and the yards at Dairycoates, a rather busy stretch of railway fraught with all sorts of mishaps waiting to happen! Whatever the circumstances behind No.69796's demise, its external appearance was a credit to 53B. This area of Botanic Gardens shed was once occupied by the coaling stage which had been superseded in the 1930s by a mechanical coaling plant. The shed itself consisted of two square roundhouses located on a north-south axis, the walls of the southernmost shed are in view immediately behind the locomotive. Built in 1901, Botanic Gardens replaced another square roundhouse type shed, which had been demolished to make space for the expansion of Paragon station. Botanic Gardens went on to become Hull's first all-diesel depot (diesel multiple units actually, with a handful of shunting locomotives) and steam was banished in June 1959 to enable rebuilding to take place to cater for the new occupants (the 1959 banishment was purely a 'paper transaction' as steam had not used the shed for some time prior to 1959). *David Dalton.*

53A & 50B – N10 No.69094 was one of eleven of its class allocated to Dairycoates, not bad considering only twenty ever existed. This somewhat grotty example, No.69094, was photographed inside No.4 shed on 26th March 1956 in the company of an ex works Ivatt Cl.4 and one of the eight ex-LMS Fowler Cl.3P 'Breadvans' just visible on the left, which were thrust upon the NE Region (Botanic Gardens were the actual recipients so this must be a visitor from 53B) during 1954/55 but were eventually sent packing from Hull in 1956. We are visiting the roundhouse prior to the massive rebuilding of all six Dairycoates roundhouses commenced in October 1956. In the event (monetary constraints came to the fore even then) only Nos.4 and 5 roundhouses survived the upheaval and were given new roofs constructed from pre-cast concrete beams and patent glazing. The other sheds were demolished but the turntables and stabling roads were left in situ as an interim measure because it was realised that the steam locomotive allocation was dwindling and nothing like the 1923 level of stabling room would be required. *David Dalton.*

56F – A 'Jubilee', two Fairburn tanks and a WD 2-8-0 – all unidentified but believed to be 45565, 42177, 42185 and 90711 – share the condemned line on the west side of Low Moor engine shed on 29th August 1966. All are recent arrivals at the 'dump' from which there was no escape. Although the WD appears to be intact, with virtually everything except its smokebox numberplate and screw coupling, its cabside window is drawn closed, a sure sign of withdrawal during the run-down of BR steam. Low Moor was one of the former Lancashire & Yorkshire Railway engine sheds which, under BR, became part of the North Eastern Region during the September 1956 boundary changes when it was re-coded 56F from its previous LMS shed code of 25F. In late August 1967 its code was changed again, this time to 55J but it was one of those non-events created to tidy-up the motive power organisation in that area of Yorkshire because just over a month later, on 2nd October 1967, the depot was closed and later demolished. *David Dalton.*

51D – When this photograph of one of the three Middlesbrough roundhouses was taken on 20th April 1958, the motley trio of sheds were not long for this world. Indeed, within less than six weeks these stalls would be empty and the whole allocation of sixty or so locomotives transferred to the new motive power depot at nearby Thornaby. This is the middle shed of the three adjoining buildings, looking north-westwards towards the 'exposed' shed with an Ivatt Class 4 just visible through the glassless arched window. The roundhouses each had 50ft turntables and dated from circa 1866 to 1869 although the last of the bunch was apparently not brought into use until 1872. These were probably the last of the true round houses to be built by the North Eastern, at a time when the largest locomotives operated by the NER were 0-6-0 tender engines; the larger, square roundhouses became the next development to shelter their motive power. This particular shed had undergone a change of roof during the early 1950s, the original pitch over each stall being replaced by the austere but functioning sloping corrugated iron clad covering; the turntables were always open to the elements negating the requirement for smoke ventilators. As if imitating their surrounding, the three 0-6-0 tank engines illustrated, J72 No.69019, J77 No.68414, and J71 No.68260, were themselves looking rather poor, externally. Amazingly, the engine sheds were not demolished until 1960! *David Dalton.*

Six years previously, on a rather wet Sunday, 27th April 1952, this was the view of Middlesbrough's open-air roundhouse viewed from the south-east quadrant. In the left background is the new extension to the general stores building. In the right background is the coaling stage, which in turn backed onto the main line. Remnants of the original engine shed roof, and walls, are represented by the open-ended pitched roof, supported by a king-post, visible in the background. Locomotives identifiable include, from left: J39s Nos.64862 and 64847, J26 No.65764 (soon to transfer to Stockton), A8 No.69860, and another, albeit unidentified J39. *David Dalton.*

Q6 No.63452 stabled on a stub road outside the general stores at the west end of the depot on Sunday 24th April 1955. The track leading into the westernmost – roofless – roundhouse is in the foreground. Overspill from the sheds saw engines using this area of the shed yard for stabling at weekends whilst the breakdown crane, just visible in the background, was kept ready in that same position for many years until closure. For orientation purposes, the new brickwork on the right belongs to an extension which is visible in the previous illustration. Resident at Middlebrough since a 14th September 1952 transfer from West Hartlepool, the Q6 dutifully moved over to Thornaby on the appointed date and ended its working life there in April 1963. *K.R.Pirt.*

56D – Although not exactly following the remit of – steam motives power depots, views of, plus locomotives therein! This Saturday 22nd January 1966 view, looking east along the Calder valley main line, shows a couple of interesting points. The first one reveals, on the south side of Mirfield engine shed yard, two independent snow ploughs, one stabled on the nearest shed road – blade towards the camera – whilst the other stands adjacent to the coaling stage. Obviously the authorities were ready for any heavy snowfall on this important cross-Pennine route and the appliances for clearing any drifting were awaiting the call. This former L&YR engine shed became part of the NE Region in 1956 and was coded 56D from thereon until closure in April 1967. Note that the coal stage is strangely quiet although still in use judging by the shiny rails on both the ramp and the coaling road. My second point concerns the passing, westbound diesel multiple unit which is one of the ubiquitous Metropolitan-Cammell types common around these parts. The ensemble appears to consist two two-car units with at least four parcels vans of the four wheel and bogie variety in tow. Now, it was not uncommon to see a d.m.u. with a single parcels vehicle coupled behind but to see four such pieces of rolling stock attached to a unit was somewhat rare. However, the NE Region apparently allowed d.m.u.s of at least four cars, and combining 1200 horsepower, to tow up to 140 tons of trailing load in the shape of parcels vehicles between Huddersfield and Leeds. In the opposite direction, because of the adverse gradients, only 80 tons was allowed. It appears that some rules might have been broken on this occasion! *David Dalton.*

29

51B – Subsidence had been a problem at Newport, North Yorkshire, since the first roundhouse built there, in 1881, had to be demolished in 1890 because it had become unsafe; in those days it must have been seriously unsafe for the NER to take such drastic action. Another engine shed, this time a twin roundhouse, was erected before demolition of the affected building took place. It is the interior of that building we are looking at as it appeared on 20th April 1958 with recently ex works Q6 No.63428 helping to illustrate a couple of points regarding said subsidence. Even then, in 1958, it was still drawing the attention of the authorities – witness the apparent incline of the Q6 tender, and the dip in the track beneath the second set of coupled wheels – but compared with 1890 nothing startling was taking place. Of course, with just weeks to go before the whole Newport allocation vacated this shed in favour of the new depot at Thornaby, the subsidence problem was about to become history. Note that the BR emblem on the tender is of the wrong-facing variety, obviously Darlington saw no reason why stocks should not be used up before they conformed to the College of Heralds instruction to use emblems with left-facing lions only. Newport's allocation consisted wholly of locomotives engaged in the movement of goods: 0-6-0, 0-8-0, 2-8-0, 0-6-0ST and 4-8-0T. *David Dalton.*

51J – Northallerton, 27th June 1954. Located alongside the Leeds-Stockton line, just west of the station serving the main line (in the left background), the engine shed consisted a two-road building with one track passing through the northern wall of the shorter section of the shed. The allocation at Northallerton at the date of the photograph was as follows: D20 – 62359; G5 – 67278, 67342; J21 – 65064; J39 – 64817, 64910, 64978; J73 – 68359; K1 – 62044, 62062; J26 – 65726. One G5 usually worked the Leyburn parcels with the other shunting Thirsk yards whilst the J21 was the stand-by engine for the latter job. Local goods work was undertaken by the three J39, with the pair of Peppercorn K1s taking turns working the Hawes pick-up goods and an evening train to York, with the other as stand-by. *David Dalton.*

Northallerton shed on 1st April 1962 with K1 No.62044 and Cl.2 No.78012. Nearly a decade on, and the BR Standard Cl.2s now have charge of the Thirsk Town goods job. Note that the K1 remains unchanged, the only survivor of the 1954 allocation. Northallerton shed was opened in 1858 by the North Eastern Railway, at first a one road shed sufficed – the building nearest the camera is believed to be the original – but in 1882 an extension, built to mirror the earlier shed, was added onto the west wall. The coaling stage and turntable were located some distance away from the shed, alongside the junction where the Stockton line joins the ECML in the Up direction. Access to those facilities from the shed was via the Stockton line, running beneath the ECML, to Northallerton Low junction, and setting back to a point on the ECML opposite the Down platform of the station – a distance of approximately half a mile! The engine shed closed on 4th March 1963 and the remaining six engines (K1 Nos.62003, 62044, with BR Cl.2 Nos.78011, 78012, 78014 and 78015) transferred to Darlington. The existing duties were then covered by Type 2 diesel locomotives from Thornaby. Note the braziers stacked by the corner of the shed; their work is done, the winter but a memory. *David Dalton.*

52E – Percy Main consisted three different engine sheds from three different dates but all of Blyth & Tyne Railway origin. The shed in view here on 22nd May 1955 was a three road, through shed which was in need of a new roof. The other sheds on the site, both dead-ended but consisting of three roads and two roads respectively, were located behind the photographer to the right, and adjacent to each other. This shed never did get a new roof but BR saw fit to install a corrugated lean-to over just one road inside the enclosure created by the stone walls; the arched gables were replaced at the same time by steel joists. Note that all the locomotives stabled on this Sunday are J27s, which is not surprising because Percy Main's allocation during most of the BR period was made up entirely of J27s! On the first day of BR there was twenty-one of the class allocated. Within a couple of years that number had risen to twenty-four only to fall back to the 1948 level by the end of the decade. But coal was their business and the nearby collieries relied on the sure footed 0-6-0s to move millions of tons every year from the pit heads to the rail heads and the shipping staithes on the Tyne. Being situated north of the Tyne, Percy Main engine shed became the diesel shunter maintenance base for the growing BR fleet during the early 1960s, the two dead-end sheds being fit for the purpose and with refuelling facilities provided. *K.R.Pirt.*

55D – Still on Huddersfield's books, WD 2-8-0 No.90680 was stored at Royston during the summer and autumn of 1966, as here on 29th August, along with three classmates. In January 1967 it was transferred to Normanton but on receipt it was condemned and sent for scrap. Considering the 'Austerity' was so prolific on the North Eastern Region, especially after the former LMS sheds came under NE Region control, we have not seen too many during our shed visits so far. *Ron Hodge.*

50E – Although the demolition of the straight shed at Scarborough took away a large slice of Scarborough's railway history, the site was still used to stable visiting diesel locomotives for some time after that event. This is the site on the afternoon of Saturday 28th May 1966, as viewed from the northernmost pedestrian entrance to the shed – situated on Seamer Road – with main line diesel locomotives awaiting their return workings. Brush, English Electric and Sulzer Type 4s dominate the former shed roads although a couple of very capable Sulzer Type 2s are also present. The scene ten years previously would have found the shed yard crammed with steam locomotives which had brought excursions and holiday extras from places such as Birmingham, Bradford, Chesterfield, Hull, Leeds, Manchester, Newcastle, Sheffield, Wigan, and even Glasgow. However, on this day diesel power appears to be the rule, and although the list of return destinations would still be fairly far flung, it would have been somewhat shorter. The vestiges of the shed's demolition litter the trackside reminding us of a period when engine sheds were being torn down all over the country and vistas changed almost weekly. The transition brought supermarkets, housing developments and car parks, leaving a vacuum which would never be 'filled' no matter what was built on the site. Note the apparent lack of smoke pollution which for many enthusiasts had been a guide to the whereabouts of 'the shed' whenever visiting a new location, usually on foot. *N.W.Skinner.*

35

Two days after the previous view was recorded on film, on Monday 30th May 1966, the same photographer ventured over to the south end of the Scarborough engine shed site and caught this group of visiting motive power. Again, it appears to be late afternoon. Remnants of the rear wall of the former shed can be seen where the floor ends abruptly in a jagged edge. At the bottom of the picture, the sloping brick wall leads to the abutment of a bridge which carried the main line over a lane which led to the gas works seen in the previous illustration. The stabled locomotives are standing on the four easternmost roads which had in fact been open to the elements since about 1957 when subsidence caused half of the engine shed to become unsafe, necessitating demolition of that portion of the eight-road building. Steam has returned to Scarborough, albeit temporarily, in the shape of a gloriously filthy 'Jubilee' No.45739 ULSTER from Wakefield. That particular engine would make a few more visits to the resort during 1966, prior to withdrawal in January 1967. In the distance can be seen the 1882 roundhouse which was still intact at this time, another steam locomotive is using the facilities at that end of the yard having turned on the 60ft table already. Also, the slope of the ramp to the former coaling stage can just be made out on the left. As was the case during the previous couple of summers, no coal was available at Scarborough in this summer of 1966 and all the depots sending out steam

36 locomotives on trains to Scarborough were instructed to fill the tenders with sufficient fuel for the return journey. *N.W.Skinner.*

The interior of the roundhouse at Scarborough. Sunday, 4th November 1962. We are looking at the south-west corner of the building which was essentially two-thirds the size of the normal NER square roundhouse. The doorway was located in what would have been the middle of the wall had the shed been of the normal dimensions. However, the west wall butted up to a steep embankment, which was topped by Seamer Road, thereby restricting the building line on that quadrant of the shed. A plan view would show what appeared to be an off-centre turntable with only two stabling stalls and two stub tracks fitting into the space on the west side (the smoke ventilators, or lack of them, help to explain the situation on that side). All the stalls on the eastern quadrant were of normal size and able to hold most of the tender engine types built for the North Eastern. Note the damp penetrating the west wall and discolouring the whitewash. The turntable was just over 44 feet in diameter and was the same unit which was laid down in 1882; it remained in situ until closure as it was deemed impossible to install a larger turntable. During BR days the shed was used mainly for repairs with the eight road straight shed used for running purposes. Also, this shed found a use as home for the couple of York-based diesel shunters which were out-stationed to Scarborough during the final years of the shed's existence. In reality, the two 0-6-0 diesel mechanical shunters, D2051 and D2268, had just joined the York complement from Dairycoates. The coming winter would find these two sheltering inside this shed on numerous occasions such was the severity of the winter and its affect on the internal combustion engine. *N.W.Skinner.*

Not a diesel in sight! Scarborough, 7th April 1957 with D49 No.62745 THE HURWORTH polluting the atmosphere. A York engine at this time, it was transferred to Scarborough in August 1958, a move which proved to be its last because in March 1959 it was condemned. Note the roof of the four-road section of shed on the left being stripped of slates ready for demolition. *David Dalton.*

(*opposite*) Ten years earlier – than the scene depicted on page 37 – on Monday 7th April 1952, Scarborough roundhouse was occupied by this solitary D20, No.62384, of Selby shed. The 4-4-0 was in winter storage and parted from its tender. No doubt the forthcoming summer timetable would see the D20 back in traffic. Note the apparent cleanliness of the roundhouse floor. *David Dalton.*

The shape of things to come at Scarborough, and elsewhere. Bristol Bath Road based Brush Type 4 D1676 VULCAN stables on the turntable outlet road at Scarborough on 29th May 1966, the time, if the wall clock was working, 1153. How this Co-Co got to Scarborough is unknown. It could have ended up here for any number of reasons and to speculate would require slightly more space than the caption allows. What is certain is that it was a Western Region engine and would remain so for some years to come. Built at Crewe, it was put into traffic at Cardiff Canton depot exactly one year before its trip to the Yorkshire coast. Named in October 1965, D1676 transferred to Bath Road depot during the previous April. *N.W.Skinner.*

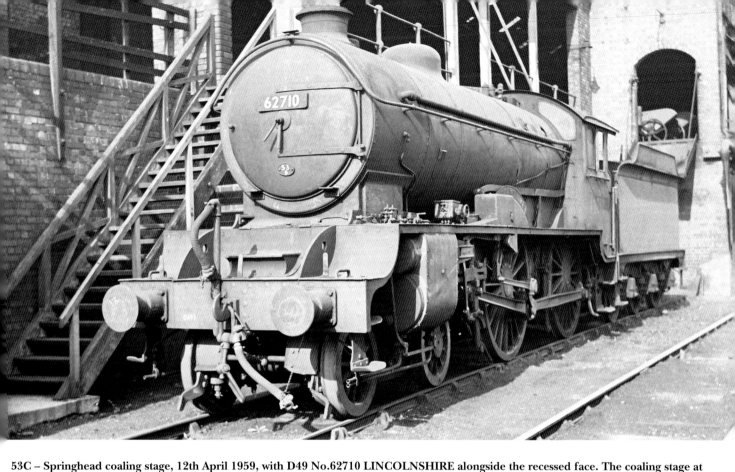

53C – Springhead coaling stage, 12th April 1959, with D49 No.62710 LINCOLNSHIRE alongside the recessed face. The coaling stage at Springhead engine shed was unusual (but not quite unique because Scarborough stage was likewise 'split') in having one of its four coaling chutes positioned on a portion of the stage which was set back and not in line with the other three. It even had its own service track on which the 4-4-0 is comfortably set for receiving fuel. However, all is not what it appears in this picture. Firstly, the D49 has a 53B shedplate but its home shed at nearby Botanic Gardens was going through the final months of a complete rip-out whereby the twin roundhouses had their turntables and stalls replaced by through trackwork to house diesel units. Officially the date of closure to steam for Botanic was June 1959 which was in fact the opening date of the rebuilt shed. The Botanic allocation, which included eight D49 at this time, not to mention a similar number of B1, along with eight Gresley V1/V3 tanks, had been virtually homeless since 1956 when work started on the rebuild. As work progressed it became harder to house the engines in the roundhouses so the facilities at Dairycoates and Springhead were used during the interim period (Dairycoates was also going through a rebuilding phase). To further complicate matters, Springhead – 53C – had closed in December 1958 but had been used to house Hull's growing band of diesel multiple units whilst work proceeded at 53B. The d.m.u fleet and the orphaned steam locomotives remained at Springhead after the closure, most of the former out on the road whilst many of the latter were put into temporary storage, including most of the D49s. No.62710 itself does not appear to be in steam in this view but the lack of sacking on the chimney indicates that all is not well and the 4-4-0 has been dumped out of the way alongside the redundant stage. This D49 was reallocated to Dairycoates when Botanic re-opened and it was put back into traffic, at least for the summer season. It even managed a couple of trips to Darlington works during August and September 1959. In and out of storage over the next twelve months, No.62710 was finally condemned during another trip to Darlington in September 1960. Springhead shed continued to be used for storage but even that came to an end in the summer of 1961 after which the demolition men moved in and the whole of the Springhead complex, shed, works and yards became history. *David Dalton.*

51E – Stockton shed, Sunday 20th April 1958 with Neville Hill B16/1 No.61412 visiting for the weekend and having resident Thompson B1 No. 61018 GNU for company. Neither engine is anywhere near clean, their appearance typifying the rapidly slipping standards of locomotive cleaning on British Railways during this decade. Both engines still had a few more years in front of them, with the pair due to undertake General overhauls in the not too distant future. The engine shed at Stockton opened in 1891, the eight-road structure replacing a smaller shed located just to the south. Typical North Eastern in design, it was equipped with all the usual facilities: turntable, coaling stage, ash pits, and water columns. In an effort to modernise the depot during the early 1950s, new pre-cast concrete inspection pits, complete with electric lighting, were laid down in front of the shed. This illustration affords us a reasonable view of one such pit with the neon lighting blazing away. For various reasons, it seems that steam locomotives and modern aids did not create a happy marriage but for the enginemen lubricating their charges, along with the fitters adjusting that last-minute task, it must have seemed like something out of a dream, at least until the dirt took hold again. Other 'aids' installed by BR included a sunken road for ash wagons which enabled ash to be tipped into wagons with greater ease than before. *David Dalton.*

Of the fifteen 4-8-0 tank engines of LNER Class T1, six had served at Stockton during various periods of their lives. Two of the five LNER built examples went new to the shed in November 1925 but in July 1930, when Stockton yard was closed during an economic downturn, the pair moved away. One of the pair however, as BR No.69919, returned to Stockton in September 1952 and ironically ended its days there, being condemned in February 1955. Four other members of the class were allocated to Stockton in BR days, amongst them our subject here which arrived from Dairycoates in September 1952 but transferred away to Selby in March 1957. Others which had resided were Nos. 69914, which had the record for the shortest stay – March to August 1955 when it went for scrap; No.69918, which had the longest stay, from March 1943 to June 1957; No.69921 from September 1955 to June 1957. Stockton's locomotive allocation was fairly cosmopolitan with no less than thirteen classes, from 4-6-0s to 0-4-4T, and 0-8-0s to 0-6-0s, allocated during BR times; as was the case when Keith Pirt captured this monster on film on Sunday 24th April 1955. Note the soot encrusted gable walls which had been subjected to sixty-four years of chimney pollution. The building itself must however have been in good condition because after the shed closed in June 1959, with the transfer of the allocation to Thornaby, it was purchased for private use and lasted a further thirty-nine years before demolition *K.R.Pirt*.

The west wall of Stockton shed on Sunday 27th April 1952, with the depot's longest serving and at that time, the only T1 allocated, No.69918, simmering in the spring drizzle. *David Dalton.*

54A & 52G – Sunderland roundhouse interior, 30th April 1967. Two resident J27s, Nos.65892 and 65833, along with a visitor from South Blyth in the shape of No.65880, appear to be hanging on to existence in a shed which was also coming to the end of its useful life. Note that the shedplates have already been removed from the smokebox doors – anything removable was deemed to be fair game by some enthusiasts but the authorities were usually one step ahead and took them off before any misdemeanour could be committed. Of the three 0-6-0s, the oldest, No.65833 from 1909, was the first to go, on the very next day in fact, Monday 1st May! South Blyth condemned their engine on 12th June whereas No.65892, a relative youngster built by the LNER in 1923, was condemned on 7th August. The shed, dating from 1875, did not last much longer and was demolished shortly after the end of steam on the NE Region. *David Dalton.*

A nice atmospheric picture of two G5s standing amidst the clutter and filth which was Sunderland engine shed in BR days. The date is 16th June 1957 and both engines are resident to 54A, No.67297 having always worked from South Dock since entering traffic sixty years previously. No.67259 was a relative newcomer having transferred from Blaydon in December 1955 for its first stay at Sunderland; it was to prove to be its final move because six months after this scene was captured on film, it was condemned. To the right is the roundhouse shed with its restrictive 42ft turntable where nothing bigger than a J27 could comfortably stable. On the left is the four road straight shed which, although hard to believe, had been rebuilt just three years previously with a new roof. *David Dalton.*

The 'staggered' four-road straight shed at Sunderland on Sunday 30th April 1967, with Q6 No.63395, Peppercorn K1 No.62012 and a couple of WD 2-8-0s hogging the stabling roads. This is another aspect of the rebuilt shed showing part of the stagger between the two pairs of tracks. All of the locomotives in view were fairly new to Sunderland depot. The Q6 had arrived in May 1965 from Darlington; Sunderland proved to be its last posting (as far as BR was concerned). A look at the back end of the tender will tell you instantly what these 0-8-0s were all about – hauling heavy, loose-coupled mineral and goods trains. The K1 had just been transferred from York that very day but was destined to last just two weeks and three days in traffic thereafter! As for the 'Austerities' – they had only become part of the Sunderland stud from August 1966 when No.90200 left Wakefield for the north-east as a sort of vanguard and was the first of twenty WD which would be allocated to 52G during 1966 and 1967. All but four of those 2-8-0s were eventually condemned at Sunderland. Along with West Hartlepool, Sunderland housed the last of steam motive power in north-east England when on 17th September 1967 both sheds closed to steam. *David Dalton.*

47

51L – The new locomotive depot at Thornaby was equipped with all that was best and new regarding steam locomotives, including this water gantry on the north side of the depot. On a date unrecorded but at some time during 1960, Q6 No.63465 has its tender tank filled, with the driver doing the honours and controlling the flow from his elevated position on the rear of the tender. Note that the 0-8-0 had already visited the coaling plant. *David Dalton.*

With the main doors still looking pristine, this is the west end of the straight shed at Thornaby on 29th September 1958, some four months after becoming operational. Even the track work appears to be new rather than salvaged – no expense, it seems, was spared for this showcase depot. The northern segment of the octagonal roundhouse pokes in from the right. The locomotives on view comprise an Ivatt Class 4 and two A8s, Nos.69891 and 69860, all from the former Middlesbrough stud, whilst the ex-WD 0-6-0ST was a representative of the erstwhile Newport shed allocation. A8 No.69891 had in fact been condemned nearly two weeks earlier and was waiting for a tow to Darlington where it was cut up soon afterwards. The other A8 still had another nine months work ahead of it before it too went to Darlington for a similar fate. The main-line diesel locomotives had still to arrive at Thornaby but when they did everything was ready for them. Meanwhile a handful of 350 h.p. 0-6-0DE shunters kept the fitters up-to-date with all things diesel, and electric! *David Dalton.*

Roundhouse interior Thornaby, circa 1960. Opened in June 1958, Thornaby depot was to be the ultimate facility for steam locomotive servicing and light maintenance. Adjacent to the roundhouse was a large straight road building with nine through roads and four dead-ended roads, built with diesel traction in mind. It was quickly and easily adapted for the new motive power prior to the banishment of steam at the end of 1964. Concrete and glass was the order of the day when it came to constructing new industrial premises in the late Fifties' and thereafter. Such materials made up the fabric of the roundhouse but the building's continued use for diesel traction was in question until it was decided to use it for their stabling. Note the nice touch of numbering each stall, the through track having no designation at all and was kept clear. Diesels did use this shed both before and after steam had vanished, and they continued to do so for some years until it was given over to wagon repairs. Demolition was carried out in 1988. *David Dalton.*

52D – The quiet, light and airy interior of the roundhouse at Tweedmouth is captured nicely in this picture taken on Sunday 2nd April 1961 with resident J72 No.68720 seemingly the only occupant of the north-west quadrant (the 52A Gateshead shed plate gives a clue to the last depot where the J72 served but that had been nearly twelve months previously!). Opened in 1877, this shed complimented a four-road straight shed which pre-dated the North Eastern Railway and which became operational in 1847. That shed, or at least the rear pedestrian entrance (besides a locomotive therein), can be seen through the arched doorway on the left. This 0-6-0T was one of those fitted in 1937 with both vacuum ejector and steam heating for carriage warming but the steam heating pipes have been removed from this end of the engine although the connection is still in situ. Note too the three-link coupling which was not changed for a screw type as this engine would only haul empty stock. The fitted open wagon in the adjacent stall possibly brought a load of sand for the Kelbus sand dryer which was located in the corner of the roundhouse, just out of sight behind the J72. However, the 40-gallon oil drums were more than likely the cargo within the wagon judging by the number illustrated. After Tweedmouth closed in 1966, the four-road straight shed was demolished but this building was purchased by a local business and may well be still in use. *David Dalton.*

54B & 52H – Long before the end of steam on British Railways, the sheds at the steam motive power depots were, in the main, nothing more than a ramshackle collection of buildings in various states of disrepair. Typical, although perhaps an extreme example, was this former North Eastern roundhouse shed – edifice – known as No.1 roundhouse at Tyne Dock. The 'shed' was little more than a ruin which had the appearance of many engine sheds found on mainland Europe after Allied bombing raids in WW2. The roof had been removed some years before this 28th January 1967 scene was captured on film, the windows too were non-existent but the overall condition of the building is nothing short of shocking. No doubt today's health and safety laws would forbid anyone entering such a building, never mind working in such a place. The hydraulic sheerlegs were one of a pair found in this particular roundhouse, another set could be found in the adjacent No.3 roundhouse. WD No.90395 appears ready to use the services of the lifting device but the 2-8-0 was in fact condemned having been withdrawn on 8th October 1966, the day it was to have been transferred to Sunderland shed! Note that it carried markings to show it was, up to that date, allocated to York shed so why it was dumped here is anyone's guess. One particular theory sees the 'Austerity' working in from York, being failed at Tyne Dock and having its tender used to keep another active WD in traffic. No.90395 was sold shortly after this event to a well-known scrap merchant in Hull. Obviously a tender of sorts was coupled for the long journey south, and whatever had caused the engine's demise initially did not necessarily impede its passage to Humberside. *David Dalton.*

Still inside that No.1 roundhouse at Tyne Dock, we have moved across the shed onto the opposite side of the turntable and the cameraman has aimed his lens towards the position from where the last picture was recorded. Again dereliction is evident but note the second set of sheerlegs which have their own shelter – wording akin to 'all mod cons' comes to mind! Some months have passed since the previous picture was taken and the sun is riding high in the sky allowing plenty of light to penetrate those gloomy corners – summer has arrived! Two of the Tyne Dock's Q6s, Nos.63429 and 63455, just about manage to stable on the seemingly inadequate stalls. Note that the track on which the right hand 0-8-0 is standing does not actually project through into the adjacent roundhouse, even though a large opening had been created at some period in the past, perhaps with view to joining up the stalls in each shed to allow through running and alternative egress. Just like the building here, the two locomotives are also coming to the end of their lives; No.63429 was condemned on 1st July 1967 whilst 63455 succumbed a week earlier. *David Dalton.*

56A – The former L&YR shed at 56A Wakefield was, during BR days, recognised as the home of the WD 2-8-0. The place was full of them with sixty or so allocated for much of the period from 1950 to closure in 1967. In this 29th August 1966 view we see three examples stabling on the shed's north yard – no doubt a walk around the premises would have revealed a couple of dozen more, all in this same deplorable external condition. Only one of the trio is identifiable as 90620, a locomotive which – excepting for a month in late 1950 – spent the whole of its life working from Wakefield and was condemned there when the shed closed. *Ron Hodge.*

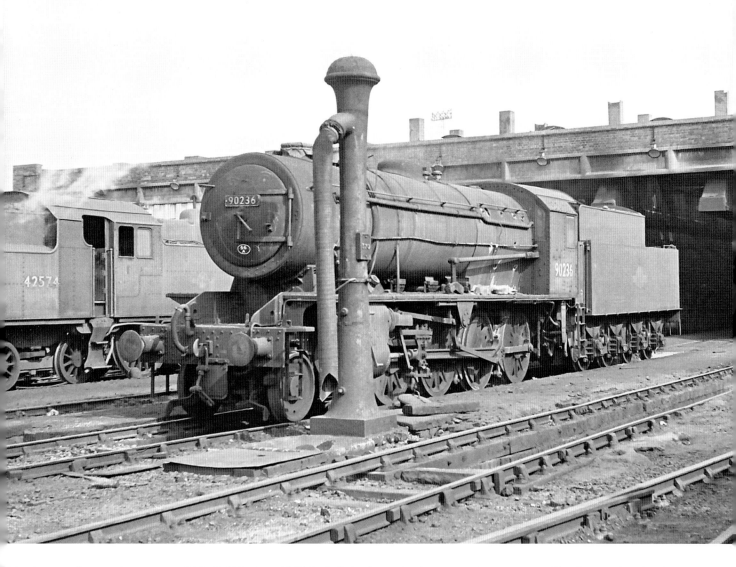

Nearly a year later and a return to Wakefield in June 1967 finds little change in the external appearance of its charges. Considering the depot was about to close, WD No.90236 still wears the 56A shedplate which, it will be noted, has been cleaned and picked-out in black and white paint but note the sacking over the chimney and the closed-to cab window! Was the 'Austerity' about to go into store or had it just come out of store? It was in fact coming out of store and was about to leave Wakefield on transfer to Normanton (17th June 1967). Whilst at Normanton it would be amongst the last steam locomotives working on the North Eastern Region and was finally condemned on 17th September 1967, a black day for steam in the north-east. This is the north end of the shed which, as can be seen, was rebuilt during the 1950s in a style adopted by the NE Region, whereby pre-cast concrete beams and cast in-situ columns were employed to support the patent glazed roof. *D.H.Beecroft.*

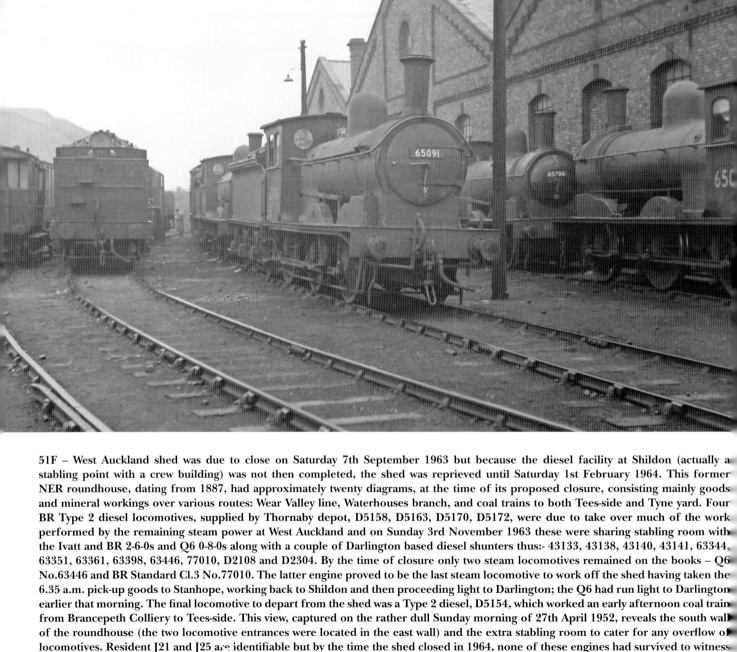

51F – West Auckland shed was due to close on Saturday 7th September 1963 but because the diesel facility at Shildon (actually a stabling point with a crew building) was not then completed, the shed was reprieved until Saturday 1st February 1964. This former NER roundhouse, dating from 1887, had approximately twenty diagrams, at the time of its proposed closure, consisting mainly goods and mineral workings over various routes: Wear Valley line, Waterhouses branch, and coal trains to both Tees-side and Tyne yard. Four BR Type 2 diesel locomotives, supplied by Thornaby depot, D5158, D5163, D5170, D5172, were due to take over much of the work performed by the remaining steam power at West Auckland and on Sunday 3rd November 1963 these were sharing stabling room with the Ivatt and BR 2-6-0s and Q6 0-8-0s along with a couple of Darlington based diesel shunters thus:- 43133, 43138, 43140, 43141, 63344, 63351, 63361, 63398, 63446, 77010, D2108 and D2304. By the time of closure only two steam locomotives remained on the books – Q6 No.63446 and BR Standard Cl.3 No.77010. The latter engine proved to be the last steam locomotive to work off the shed having taken the 6.35 a.m. pick-up goods to Stanhope, working back to Shildon and then proceeding light to Darlington; the Q6 had run light to Darlington earlier that morning. The final locomotive to depart from the shed was a Type 2 diesel, D5154, which worked an early afternoon coal train from Brancepeth Colliery to Tees-side. This view, captured on the rather dull Sunday morning of 27th April 1952, reveals the south wall of the roundhouse (the two locomotive entrances were located in the east wall) and the extra stabling room to cater for any overflow of locomotives. Resident J21 and J25 are identifiable but by the time the shed closed in 1964, none of these engines had survived to witness the event. However, this depot had been closed once before, in 1931, when the LNER was trying survive an economic downturn but in the summer of 1935 it was re-opened for business once again. There would be no such escape in 1964 because the shed was demolished shortly after closure. The age of the roundhouse was over! *David Dalton.*

Just a little further up the yard, at the rear of the shed at West Auckland, a mound of colliery waste overlooked proceedings and also gave a clue as to the predominant industry in this area. The shed, of course, catered for the requirements of the coal industry – in good times and bad – with the allocation consisting almost two-thirds goods engines. On Sunday 27th June 1954, J21 No.65062 and Y1 Sentinel No.68145 stable at the west end of the yard for the weekend break but the sixty-four years old 0-6-0 is now living on borrowed time and by the end of the year it was condemned and scrapped. The little Sentinel however, after a further year at West Auckland, moved down to the coast (well nearly) at Dairycoates but less than a year later it transferred to the seaside proper, at Bridlington; the semi-retirement did not last long however because in January 1957, whilst on a visit to Darlington works, it was condemned. *David Dalton.*

51F – Twelve years on from the scene depicted on page 1, and Q6 No.63344 and WD No.90339 stand at the south end of the straight shed at West Hartlepool on 22nd July 1967. The gable wall of the shed has by now been shored-up; old age, mining subsidence or a combination of both, being responsible for its precarious existence. The roof of the place looks rather dubious too but the only money to be expended on this building was for its imminent demolition which was not too far away. The Austerity had been withdrawn three weeks previously (note the closed cab window) whilst the 0-8-0 is steaming away ready for its next duty. A newcomer to 51C in September 1966, the WD had come from Wakefield and the eagle-eyed amongst you will spot the faded 'polo' beneath the number on the cabside signifying that it was once one of Wakefield's finest! The days of this depot, along with its allocation, were numbered – within two months steam workings would cease and the few diesel locomotives using the yard to stable would move on. *Ron Hodge.*

Looking across the yard of the old wagon shop towards West Hartlepool's straight shed as a WD 2-8-0 heads south with a loaded coal train in July 1967. This picture of dereliction – the former wagon works, which had been inoperative for some years, was in much better condition than the engine shed – sums up nicely the motive power accommodation available (Thornaby apart) in these latter months of North Eastern steam on BR. *Ron Hodge.*

Q6 No.63438 and G5 No.67272 block the entrance and exit roads to the roundhouse sheds at West Hartlepool on Sunday 27th April 1952. These openings were the only means of entry into the two roundhouses here and prior to WW2, only the right hand, arched, opening was available. The left hand opening, with the concrete lintel, was an afterthought to help prevent the possible stranding of forty or so locomotives in the event of an incident occurring on this single artery. We are looking at the 1871 roundhouse which, as can be seen, has had its central roof pitch re-clad in corrugated materials, the original slates and their fixings having given up. *David Dalton.*

West Hartlepool coaling stage, Saturday 8th September 1956. J72 No.68703 and A8 No.69893, both residents of 51C, were being replenished prior to their weekend sojourn on shed. Note that the working face of the stage is completely open to the elements whereas some of these manual stages had corrugated iron (see Heaton for instance) or even timber cladding fitted to keep out the wind; in West Hartlepool's case the wind was mainly blowing from the rear of the stage, straight off the North Sea and therefore predominately a cold easterly'! *David Dalton.*

50G – The picturesque setting of Whitby attracted numerous enthusiasts over the years and on 22nd February 1953 a small coach party of visitors make their way around the two road shed with the dying rays of sunlight casting shadows over the scene. Visiting A5 No.69888 and G5 No.67289 hog the yard whilst two resident engines lurk inside the shed. *David Dalton.*

WHITBY - *A potted history of the engine shed*:

The original one road York & North Midland Railway engine shed, dating from 1847, was enlarged in 1868 into a two-road dead ended shed which lasted until closure by British Railways on 6th April 1959. LNER facilities included a 60ft turntable installed in 1936 to replace a 50ft example put in by the North Eastern Railway to replace the original 42ft example. A coal stage, with a steam powered crane, sufficed throughout the twentieth century. Being as it was somewhat isolated, the shed was equipped with sheerlegs, fitting staff and a boilersmith. The shed building was still in private use until 2000 and may still be standing.

Allocation: The BR Period:

The first day of the British Railways era found ten locomotives allocated to Whitby shed, somewhat less than the seventeen which took the shed into LNER ownership twenty-five years earlier. The Grouping allocation consisted twelve tank engines and five goods tender engines. On 1st January 1948 the numbers were different but the proportional share was similar with seven tank and three goods tender engines represented by five G5's, one A6, one A8 and three J24's. During the year three of the G5's were ousted along with the A6, whilst one of the J24's went for scrap. Another A6 came to help out with the summer traffic but left in October. In came one J24 as a replacement for the condemned engine but no less than six A8's arrived too although one was only a temporary posting and left in mid July.

The following year found three of the depot's J24's condemned but four others were drafted in from far and wide. In a straight swap one G5 left as another arrived. In and out during 1949 was J25 No.65708, from Darlington shed, which came in November but left four weeks later for York shed. The J24's allocated to Whitby had responsibility for clearing accumulated snow especially from the high routes radiating out of the town. For these duties at least two of them were fitted with snow ploughs each autumn, ready for the possible winter blizzards and inevitable drifting. In 1949, Nos.5624 and 65628 were fitted out at Gateshead works for the job.

In 1950 all four of Whitby's J24's were withdrawn along with No.5631 which had arrived in October and was condemned in November. Taking the place of the ancient 0-6-0's were a pair of J27's from a class which had only ever had one representative at Whitby before, and that in the 1930's. In June one of the A8's was replaced by two others whilst No.69882 came and went in the latter months of the year. There was very little movement in 1951 but the shed lost on of its A8's along with a J27. Coming in were a J25 and another J27 to keep the balance. During the late summer J27 No.65883 came and went after covering for one of its kind in works.

The highlight of 1952 occurred when Q6 No.63440 came from Selby in mid-October and hung around until four days before Christmas when it returned from whence it came. Two J27's went in June and Whitby received two J25's in their place whilst in May another A8 joined the six already allocated. The end of 1953 was very much like the start of that year with seven A8's, two G5's and three J25's allocated. Comings and goings during the year had another Q6, No.63378, visiting, this one coming for the summer but leaving on 1st November. Also for the summer season an A8 was borrowed from Neville Hill.

Although 1954 was very quiet with one A8 leaving and a J25 arriving (not to mention the same A8 once again borrowed from Leeds), 1955 turned out to be a somewhat expansive year in many ways. Five of the former NER engines were transferred out and a veritable multitude of 'new blood' arrived on the premises. Brand new in June and July were five BR Standard Cl.4 tank engines of the 2-6-4 variety, with consecutive numbers 80116 to 80120, and set to oust out all of the older motive power. These were followed by four BR Standard 2-6-0 tender engines of Class 3 but one of those left before years end. Next in was a BR built 2-6-4T of LMS design, No.42083. The final newcomer was J25 No.65687 which arrived in time for the winter season. Another J25 came and went during the year.

So the New Years day of 1956 found a rather modern looking stud of engines gracing the stabling roads at Whitby shed with eight BR Standards, a BR built 2-6-4T, four A8's, a G5 and two J25's – sixteen engines in all, the largest allocation in years. Surprisingly, only one withdrawal took place in 1956 when G5 No.67302 was condemned in April. Three transfers away took place affecting an A8, J25, and one of the Standards. This brought the numbers down to a less extravagant dozen. Coming in and then leaving three months later were two more of the BR built LMS designed 2-6-4T's, whilst three engines left temporarily and returned during the same spring period.

1957 seemed quiet by comparison to the previous two years. One J25 came in as another left whilst one of the A8's departed also. In January Middlesbrough sent two Thompson L1's but then went back north in March. The following year found the three remaining NER designed engines, two A8's and a single J25, all withdrawn and sent off to Darlington for scrap. Six of the BR Standards went too and losing nine locomotives could only mean one thing – closure was around the corner. As a consolation, the two LMS 2-6-4 tanks, which had a fleeting visit in 1956, were drafted in with one Standard 2-6-0. So, by years end the allocation stood at five engines: 42083, 42084, 42085, 77004 and 77013 – not a whiff of LNER anywhere, never mind North Eastern!

The inevitable happened on 5th April 1959 when the five 'foreigners' were transferred away and the depot closed for good, it's work completed after one hundred and twelve years. Coincidentally, one hundred and twelve different locomotives and Sentinel railcars had been allocated to Whitby shed since the start of the LNER – 1/1/23.

BR Period allocations at Whitby – a summary – 1/1/48 to closure:

Loco. No.	From	Dates	To.
A6 CL:			
9792	Starbeck	5/10/47-30/5/48	Starbeck.
9799	Starbeck	15/8/48-31/10/48	Starbeck.
A8 CL:			
69852	Starbeck	12/3/45-4/6/50.	West Hartlepool.
69858	Middlesbrough	30/5/48-29/6/54	Neville Hill.
69860	Middlesbrough	30/5/48-25/9/55	Hull Botanic Gdns.
69861	Sunderland	4/6/50-21/10/51	Selby.
	Selby	11/5/52-3/6/56	Malton.
69864	West Hartlepool	4/6/50-29/10/58c	Scrap.
69865	Blaydon	30/5/48-21/4/58c	Scrap.
69880	Middlesbrough	30/5/48-11/7/48	Middlesbrough.
69882	Scarborough	1/10/50-19/11/50	Neville Hill.
	Neville Hill	19/7/53-20/9/53	Neville Hill.
	Neville Hill	6/6/54-19/9/54	Neville Hill.
69888	Middlesbrough	30/5/48-25/9/55	Hull Botanic Gdns.
69890	Hull Botanic Gdns	15/8/48-19/2/56	York.
	York	10/6/56-30/6/57	Malton.
G5 CL:			
67240	Neville Hill	19/7/53-20/11/55	Malton.
67262	Malton	7/7/41-6/6/48	Neville Hill.
67293	Malton	29/9/46-30/1/49	Neville Hill.
67302	Residen	1/1/23-26/12/48	Neville Hill.
	Neville Hill	30/1/49-10/4/56c	Scrap.
67308	Malton	28/3/42-6/6/48	Neville Hill.
67335	Resident	1/1/23-10/8/53c	Scrap.
J24 CL:			
65609	Tyne Dock	12/5/46-5/10/49c	Scrap.
5612	York	30/12/38-14/2/48c	Scrap.
5621	York	31/7/49-4/9/50c	Scrap.
5624	Newport	30/11/49-13/9/50c	Scrap.
5627	Borough Gardens	30/11/49-5/12/50c	Scrap.
65628	Malton	26/6/49-20/11/50c	Scrap.
65629	South Blyth	21/6/39-2/5/49c	Scrap.
5631	Malton	1/10/50-21/11/50c	Scrap.
65633	Borough Gardens	15/2/48-11/4/49c	Scrap.

Loco. No.	From	Dates	To.
J25 CL:			
65647	Selby	15/6/52-25/9/55	York.
65648	Neville Hill	16/6/57-30/9/58c	Scrap.
65663	Selby	8/6/52-16/6/57	Hull Dairycoates.
65675	Selby	28/11/54-23/1/55	York.
65685	Malton	23/1/55-25/9/55	York.
65687	York	13/11/55-10/6/56	Heaton.
65690	Hull Dairycoates	7/1/51-18/11/54c	Scrap.
65708	Darlington	10/11/49-11/12/49	York.
J27 CL:			
65857	Saltburn	10/12/50-15/6/52	Selby.
65883	York	29/7/51-9/9/51	York.
65887	Stockton	10/12/50-29/7/51	York.
65888	York	29/7/51-15/6/52	Selby.
L1 CL:			
67763	Middlesbrough	7/1/57-2/3/57	Middlesbrough.
67765	Middlesbrough	7/1/57-3/3/57	Middlesbrough.
Q6 CL:			
63378	Selby	3/5/53-1/11/53	Selby.
63440	Selby	12/10/52-21/12/52	Selby.
LMS Cl.4. 2-6-4T:			
42083	Darlington	25/9/55-5/4/59	Sowerby Bridge.
42084	Scarborough	12/2/56-6/5/56	Scarborough.
	Scarborough	8/6/58-5/4/59	Springs Branch.
42085	Scarborough	12/2/56-6/5/56	Scarborough.
	Scarborough	8/6/58-5/4/59	Darlington.
BR Standard Cl.3. 2-6-0:			
77004	Darlington	25/9/55-6/11/55	Darlington.
	York	21/9/58-5/4/59	Neville Hill.
77012	West Auckland	6/11/55-7/12/58	York.
77013	Darlington	25/9/55-5/4/59	Neville Hill.
77014	Darlington	25/9/55-6/6/56	Blaydon.
BR Standard Cl.4. 2-6-4T:			
80116	York	15/5/55-12/2/56	Scarborough.
	Scarborough	6/5/56-8/6/58	Neville Hill.
80117	New	19/5/55-8/6/58	Neville Hill.
80118	New	15/6/55-8/6/58	Neville Hill.
80119	New	21/6/55-12/2/56	Scarborough.
	Scarborough	6/5/56-8/6/58	Neville Hill.
80120	New	6/7/55-8/6/58	Neville Hill.

50A – Running-in after completing a General overhaul at Darlington, Heaton allocated V2 No.60922 called in at York shed in August 1959 prior to working back to Darlington and eventually home. The 2-6-2 is standing at the north end of the Clifton (York North) shed and would appear to be making its way to the turntable prior to filling its tender at the coaling plant which was located just behind the photographer. Of all former LNER engine sheds, York had the highest number of V2s allocated throughout the BR period and in 1959, when their numbers at 50A were declining, some twenty-eight of the class resided. Although never allocated to York, No.60922 was no stranger to the place and often worked in from the various sheds it called home during its twenty-three years lifetime. No doubt it called in at York for one last time whilst en route to Swindon for scrapping during the summer of 1964. *K.R.Pirt.*

Peppercorn A1 No.60140 BALMORAL has just replenished its tender at York coaling plant on Sunday afternoon, 1st September 1963. Already the growing ECML diesel fleet is not just taking over many of the principal expresses but they are also encroaching on the valuable stabling space at the motive power depots. Witness the group of English Electric and BR Sulzer Type 4s on the sidings surrounding the turntable in the distance. King's Cross and Grantham sheds have become history and facilities for the steam locomotive south of Doncaster are becoming non-existent. York meanwhile managed to keep its steam fleet going, and would do for some years to come. No.60140, for instance, kept going until January 1965 but other Pacifics lasted longer. The coaling plant is showing its age with spalling of the concrete evident in this view. Nowadays such an event would have a building cordoned-off and probably condemned but BR managed to get away with hundreds of cases of dangerous building dilapidation without anyone raising an eyebrow, at least not officially. Many of the buildings featured in this album were on the verge of gradual and total collapse but we as enthusiasts did not let such things bother us; neither, I seems, did the personnel who had to work in such surroundings. *David Dalton.*

Although the main line diesels at York were stabled away from the running sheds, their maintenance was taken care of alongside the steam locomotives within the straight road shed. On 13th December 1964 an English Electric Type 4 and a diesel mechanical shunter were sharing the repair shed with Peppercorn A1 No.60145 SAINT MUNGO. The latter is apparently having a piston examination which will help keep it in traffic for some time to come – see also Darlington. *David Dalton.*

Okay, HARDWICKE would look good there, with TOMMY alongside and perhaps EVENING STAR next to that! It was only ten years after this scene was captured on film that the staff of the NRM would have been planning their display in the Great Hall on this very spot, or thereabouts! York roundhouse, 9th May 1965 with A1s Nos.60155 BORDERER and 60138 BOSWELL keeping company with an exiled 9F from the Western Region, No.92231. *David Dalton.*

It wasn't all Pacifics and big locomotives at York North shed in the Sixties'. On 9th May 1965 two of York's eleven remaining V2s, Nos.60810 and 60895, share shed space with ex works J27, No.65894, which had recently returned from a General overhaul at Darlington. In the seventeen years since Nationalisation, the steam locomotive population at York had dropped to a third of the 1948 level; the V2s themselves were reflecting a similar reduction but one of the most dramatic declines was in the allocation of B16s which had been sixty-nine – all of the class – when BR came into being, to nil by 1964! Of course at that time only a couple of Peppercorn A2 Pacifics called this place home whereas in 1965, seven of the same CMEs' A1s were resident. This shed had been rebuilt during the previous decade but the soot blackened roof gave no hint as to that event ever taking place. However, one highlight of this picture is the J27 itself which moved to Sunderland in October 1966 and was chosen by the North Eastern Locomotive Preservation Group for preservation. *David Dalton.*

A nice study of front ends at York on Saturday 9th April 1966 with Thompson B1 No.61199, and Peppercorn K1s Nos.62028 and 62065 showing off detail and the many differences. A few of the more obvious examples are, for instance – works plates. All have them attached to the same location on the frames, but the B1 had the North British Locomotive Co. diamond shaped plate (works number 26100 of June 1947), whilst the K1s, which were from the same builder, and incidentally the same works – Queens Park – had oval plates applied (26632 of August 1949 and 26669 of January 1950 respectively). All three had acquired the British Railways AWS but for some reason the shedplate is missing from the 4-6-0; after its recent (October 1965) transfer from Tyne Dock was probably considered as not worth bothering to fit a plate because, at that time, the growing fleet of main-line diesels being acquired by 50A perhaps had priority over what got what! *David Dalton.*